Happiness Advantage

Be Your Better Self and Achieve Success
Through Happiness

Chloe S

Table of Contents

Introduction

I want to thank you and congratulate you for purchasing the book, *"Happiness Advantage"*.

This book contains proven steps and strategies on how to "Be your Better Self and Achieve Success through Happiness".

The research into happiness over the last 30 years has deepened our insight into what it means to be happy and also how to achieve happiness. Recently, the research has shown that happiness is not a result of success but that in fact the opposite is true.

Happiness leads to success.

Drawing on a large number of studies that explore happiness and success, this book seeks to draw out some of the practical lessons so that you can choose your own happiness.

Happiness Advantage

Learning techniques to become happier will help you enjoy life more and help you achieve your goals! Get started today and you'll see results within weeks.

Thanks again for purchasing this book, I hope you enjoy it!

Section 1:
Happiness and success

Conventional wisdom states that to be happy we need to have a successful career, a loving family, a good income and a healthy body. Consequently, many of us spend our lives chasing that smiling carrot that always seems to be just out of reach.

- If I lose a little weight, I'll be happy.

- If I get that promotion, I'll be happy.

- If I find the perfect partner, I'll be happy.

- If I get better grades, I'll be happy.

But it turns out that, in fact, the link between happiness and success is the other way around.

Happiness Advantage

Happiness drives success

"Your brain at positive performs significantly better than at negative, neutral or stressed," says Shawn Achor in his massively successful Ted Talk on the *Happy Secret to Better Work*[i].

Research study after research study has proven that the key to success is being happy.

When we are happy we are more creativity, energetic, productive, efficient and resilient. A positive attitude helps us deal with stress in a constructive way and allows us to see difficulties as challenges, not threats.

This is because, while negative emotions, like fear, narrow our focus and limits our actions (so that our ancestors could get away from tigers and bears without being distracted), positive emotions make us open to possibilities and new ideas. At the same time, positive emotions help us recharge and develop our personal resource[ii].

What is happiness?

When experts talk about happiness, what do they mean? Is the guy at the office who always clowns around happy? Is the mom at school who exudes calm and peace happy? Are you happy?

Barbara Fredrickson[iii] is one of the early positive psychology researchers. She started her research into positive emotions in the late '90s and has broken down positivity into "the big 10 emotions", namely: love, joy, gratitude, serenity, interest, hope, pride, amusement, inspiration and awe. In some sense happiness, (or as Frederickson prefers to call it "positivity"), is a combination of some or all of these emotions.

In their research, many academics define happiness to mean when a person has "satisfaction and meaning in their life". It's not a passing emotion, rather it's an inclination to feel positive emotions like "the big 10". It's also about being able to recover quickly from negative emotions.

Psychiatrist Manfred Spitzer says, "Long-term happiness has a lot to do with purpose and meaning and very little with consumption or gratification.[iv]"

So are you happy? Are you more or less happy than you were last month? Are you happier than your neighbor?

These questions are difficult to answer because happiness is inherently subjective. No-one can really compare your experience of happiness to anyone else's.

It's true that there are some objective measures of happiness; the levels of cortisol in your body for example, which areas of your brain are seen to be active in a brain scan, or how many times you smile in a given period of time. Scientists use these indicators when conducting happiness studies, but for the most part they rely on how participants say they feel.

So how happy are you? And do you practice happiness skills in your daily life?

There are various online tools, questionnaires and mobile apps that can help you gauge your own level of happiness and any change in your positive state. For example, the organization Pursuit of Happiness[v] has a skills quiz to test your daily happiness practices. Dave Sze at the Huffington Post explains how to track your own subjective wellbeing over time. Or you could try the Tactics for Happier Living quiz.

Researchers often try to measure what they call "subjective well-being". This usually involves asking people a range of questions that help the researcher understand their level of life satisfaction and their emotional experience.

To develop understand different aspects of happiness and develop reliable insights, researchers need to explore happiness using different methods. If studies using different research techniques all come to the same conclusion, then you can be fairly certain that the conclusions can be relied on.

Researchers in various disciplines, including psychology, psychiatry, economics and other health sciences, have designed studies to explore positivity, each study providing a little more insight into happiness, how it's experienced, what causes it and how you can create it.

Studies into happiness can be broken into four major types[vi], which tend to observe or measure different aspects of happiness:

- Observation & experience sampling studies look at how people feel at a specific moment.

- Cross-sectional/correlation studies survey how people say they feel at one moment in time by answering various questions.

- Longitudinal studies are used to observe people's lives over time to find the trajectory of a happy life.

- Experimental studies try to find causal links between happiness and outside sources.

The positivity studies that have adopted these methods are starting to show a rich and nuanced understanding of the interplay between happiness, physical changes in the body and the brain, and behavior. We are starting to see how happiness forms part of a complex system.

While there are still many aspects of happiness that we don't fully understand, there are some key conclusions that are now well-accepted. That happiness precedes success and predicts success is one of these.

Make yourself happy

It's all good and well understanding that happiness leads to success. But what if I'm just not a particularly happy person? Am I doomed to live a life of mediocrity? The good news is that happiness is something that we can all work on.

To some degree your level of happiness is determined by your DNA and your circumstances, but to a surprising degree, your happiness depends on you. As psychologists have come to understand what characteristics and behaviors help people to be happy, they have devised programs and advice to help people take control of their own happiness. And consequently their own success.

So now, instead of putting all our energy into trying to be more successful, we need to start looking at how to be happier. We spend a great deal of time and effort making sure that our CVs are professional, that our projects are completed on time, and that we network with the right people. It's time to shift some of that effort to making ourselves happier.

Happiness Advantage

Through this book, you will learn techniques and strategies that you can implement from day-to-day to make you a more positive person. And as you internalize a positive attitude, your behaviors in all areas of your life will change for the better.

Don't be daunted! While a few of the techniques we'll be looking at involve a level of long-term commitment and perseverance, many are so quick and easy to do that you can do them during your commute to the office, or while you're packing away your groceries.

You will also see the results quickly. Keep the perfect journal, and in just five days you can feel the difference. Take on the 21 day happiness advantage challenge and you experience sustained happiness within a month.

But before we look at how you can create your own happiness, let's look a bit deeper into what happiness looks like amongst successful people.

Section 2:

The Happiness advantage

Apart from the fact that happiness makes us, well, happy, there are numerous other benefits to be enjoyed.

You see, happiness triggers chemical processes in our bodies (dopamine and serotonin release) that prime the learning centers of our brains and make us more open to new experiences and information. A happy brain is better able to organize new information, store that information and make it easier to retrieve later. It is also better able to make neural connections. These connections speed up our processing powers, turn on our creativity, help us become more analytical, aid us in problem solving, and enable us to see things in a new and innovative ways[vii].

As various authors have noted, happy individuals are successful across multiple life domains, including marriage, friendship, income, work performance, and health[viii]. Happy people are physically and mentally healthier, more successful at learning and work, more creative, more popular, more sociable, less likely to be criminal or addicted, and they live longer[ix]. Happiness makes people more sociable, more altruistic, better able to resolve conflict, healthier, and more accepting of themselves[x]. Happy people are less egoistic, less aggressive, less abusive to others and less prone to illness[xi].

Happiness Benefits

"More than any other element, fun is the secret of Virgin's success."

Richard Branson

There is a very wide range of possible success outcomes when you are happy. But what does it mean to say, for example, "Happiness will make you more successful at learning"?

Let's unpack some of these outcomes in more detail to get a better understanding of just how big an impact happiness can have on our lives.

Happiness boosts productivity and performance

Let's start in the workplace.

Various studies have been done to determine just how much more productive, effective and efficient a happy worker is than his or her peers.

In one productivity study, volunteers who ate chocolate and watched a funny video completed 10-12% more math problems that volunteers who watched a neutral video beforehand (without any delicious snacks)[xii].

Another study, by renowned positivity psychologist Martin Seligman, showed that happy employees are more likely to get better performance evaluations and higher pay.[xiii]

A 15-year-long study of young people showed that happier participants were more likely to have gainful employment and higher income.

What's more happy employees have lower medical costs, work more efficiently and are absent less often[xiv].

Happiness Advantage

In his book *Happiness Advantage*, Shawn Achor reports from studies his team have done that,

"When the human brain is positive ... Productive energy rises by 31 percent. The likelihood of promotion rises by 40 percent. Sales rise by 37 percent."

It's useful to note that in the context of productivity studies, you need to distinguish between happiness meaning personal well-being, and job satisfaction. The research into job satisfaction and productivity has very mixed results[xv].

Happiness improves learning

Happiness and learning have a wonderful, mutual relationship. Learning new things can help you become happier, and when you are happier you are better able to learn.

Studies have shown that there is a link between happiness and Grade Point Average (GPA) for students. Why would this be?

Imagine a classroom of students, anxious, withdrawn, and disengaged. These learners are essentially in a fight or flight mode. Their brains are in a narrow, guarded state. This is not the mode for learning.

Bring some fun and happiness into the class, and the learners adopt a more positive attitude. The brain abandons its threat response, dopamine levels increase, and a very special part, deep down in the center of the brain, activates.

This is the *nucleus accumbens*. Whether it's chocolate, exercise, laughter, friendship or sex, positive emotions make your *nucleus accumbens* light up.

In the 1950s, experiments showed that rats would push a button to stimulate this part of their brain to the exclusion of all other activity, including eating and sleeping. They ultimately died because nothing else was as satisfying as pushing that button.

For a long time, no-one understood what the purpose was of this part of the brain. We know that positivity activates it, but why? We now know that it is linked to learning. When the *nucleus accumbens* is activated we learn better, and because we are learning in a positive environment, we learn about the things that are good for us.

A positive brain broadens the number of possibilities we process, makes us more thoughtful, creative and open to new ideas. This allows us to develop intellectual, social and physical resources for the future. Positivist psychologist Barbara Fredrickson has termed this the "Broaden and Build Theory."

Dr. David Rock, co-founder of the NeuroLeadership Institute puts it like this,

"There is a large and growing body of research which indicates that people experiencing positive emotions perceive more options when trying to solve problems, solve more non-linear problems that require insight, [and they] collaborate better and generally perform better overall."[xvi]

Happiness not only improves our ability to learn, we can also use learning to boost our happiness. [xvii] This is because the *nucleus accumbens* isn't interested in the familiar. It wants new and exciting stimulus.

In the section on techniques to make yourself happier, you'll find out more about how to use learning to promote positivity.

Happiness fosters creativity

In the same way, that positivity supports learning, it also supports creativity.

Researchers from the University of Toronto, exploring the link between happiness and creativity, used specially selected music to affect the participants' mood. Then they asked them to do two tests. The group of happy participants were better able to solve the creativity puzzle, than the other groups. However, the happy participants were less successful on the other task which required single-minded focus.

Researcher Adam Anderson explains, "With positive mood, you actually get more access to things you would normally ignore ... Instead of looking through a porthole, you have a landscape or panoramic view of the world."

Harvard researchers[xviii] have similarly also found that creativity is less likely to be present with negative emotions such as fear, anger, sadness, and anxiety. Instead it is associated with positive emotions such as joy, love, and curiosity.

Happiness improves health

There are numerous ways in which happiness promotes physical health. Daisy Coyle at HealthLine has summarized some of the evidence[xix].

Firstly, happiness supports healthier lifestyle choices, like eating more healthily and getting more exercise.

- Adults who are happier have been found to be 47% more likely to eat fresh fruits and vegetables than less positive adults[xx].

- Happy people are also 33% more likely to be physically active[xxi].

- Happy people have far fewer sleep problems than people with low levels of positive well-being[xxii].

Happiness has also been shown to boost the immune system, helping you fight off infections. For example, a study which exposed volunteers to the rhino and influenza viruses, found that volunteers with a positive emotional style were much less likely to contract the virus than their less happy counterparts[xxiii].

Section 2: The Happiness advantage

Happiness reduces your stress levels. A number of studies have found that happier people have lower levels of cortisol (the stress hormone) in their bodies. In a stressful moment, happy people produce less cortisol[xxiv] and this effect seems to persist over time[xxv].

A positive attitude reduces your blood pressure and in so doing protects your heart. Various studies have found that happiness is linked to lower blood pressure and also to lower risk of heart disease. However the evidence is mixed and further research is needed in this area.

Believe it or not, happiness can actually help reduce pain. Studies into arthritis[xxvi] and stroke recovery[xxvii] have shown that people with positive well-being may experience less pain.

And to top it all off, a positive outlook can lead to a longer life. A number of large scale studies have shown a distinct link between happiness and greater life expectancy. One study involving 32 000 people found that unhappy individuals were 14% more likely to die during the 30 year-long study than happy ones[xxviii].

Section 3:
Characteristics of happy people

Shawn Achor is a positivity psychologist who has studied people's happiness for years at Harvard University. His research has been key in showing that success follows happiness and not the other way around. His Ted Talk and book "The Happiness Advantage" have been massively popular and have made choosing happiness the talk of the town.

His numerous studies have shown that successful people share three key characteristics. According to Achor's studies these characteristics account for 75% of people's success in the workplace. Intelligence and technical skills make up the remaining 25%.

Achor notes, "If we can get somebody to raise their levels of optimism or deepen their social connection or raise happiness, turns out every single business and educational outcome we know how to test for improves dramatically."

So what are these amazing characteristics that we should all strive for?

- An optimistic outlook

- Perceiving an obstacle as a challenge not a threat

- Social connections

And while it's not easy to just through off your old ways and adopt a new positive approach, it is possible to shift your level of optimism, learn how to see challenges differently and build your social connections.

Optimism

"A pessimist sees the difficulty in every opportunity; an optimist sees the opportunity in every difficulty."

-- Winston Churchill

Are you a glass half full, or a glass half empty person?

An optimistic person sees the glass as half full and approaches the world with hope and confidence, always expecting a favorable outcome. This doesn't mean that they are naïve or blind to possible risks, but rather that they view and plan for these in a positive way.

Research shows that there are enormous benefits to being optimistic. People this kind of outlook tend to:

- be healthier[xxix] and live longer[xxx],

- be happier[xxxi],

- be more resilient[xxxii],

- better performance[xxxiii].

And while optimism has been shown to help protect against depression and various medical problems, like heart disease[xxxiv], pessimism has been linked with mood disorders, stress, and anxiety[xxxv].

In some ways optimism is a self-fulfilling prophecy. If you expect people to like you, people are more likely to like you. If you expect a negotiation to go well, you are more likely to be happy with the result[xxxvi].

But don't confuse a positive view of the future with blind faith. Just believing in a wonderful outcome will not make it magically appear.

Contrary to popular belief, visualizing your dream outcome is not going to make it happen[xxxvii]. There is a large body of research that shows that only visualizing your ideal in fact has the opposite effect. People who rely on visualization don't put in the effort needed to make things happen.

Similarly standing in front of the mirror and repeating upbeat mantras is not going to make you more optimistic.

Don't worry though, there are proven techniques that can help you shift to a more positive frame of mind.

Learn to see problems as fleeting, limited and not your fault.

To train yourself to be more optimistic you need to adjust the way you see each situation.

Section 3: Characteristics of happy people

If something bad happens, do you always think it was your fault? When you encounter a setback, do you think that it's going to hold you back forever? When things don't go your way, do regard it as a giant catastrophe that is going to affect every area of your life?

If you're a pessimist then you probably answered yes to all these questions. Optimists on the other hand, tend to look at a negative situation and think that bad things are temporary, have specific causes, and are not their fault (at least not entirely)[xxxviii].

And when good things happen, optimists perceive the positive situation as being long lasting, far reaching and brought about by their own actions. While pessimists think that good things are fleeting, rare and random.

To move from one camp into the other, the trick is to listen to the voice in your head that tells you that a negative event is a total disaster (pervasive) that it will last forever (permanent) and that it is all your fault (personal). Turn that story upside down!

The voice in your head says, "I've messed up and everybody is furious with me and now I am never going to get a promotion!"

Ask yourself: Is absolutely everybody really furious at you? Is this one mistake really going to outweigh all the good work you've done in the past? Was it entirely your fault?

It's sometimes useful to imagine someone else standing in your shoes. If your colleague was in this situation, would you really tell them that it was all their fault and that the consequences would be long term and catastrophic?

Probably not. We are better able to view events in an objective light when we are not directly involved. So do a little thought experiment and take yourself out of the equation. Every time you hear that negative self-talk, try to put the situation into perspective and adopt a more optimistic attitude.

Seeing challenges not threats

A specific optimistic trait that happy people share is that they tend to redefine stress as a challenge rather than as a threat, and face demanding situations constructively and with a positive attitude.

These people see challenges as an opportunity to learn, grow, improve or change, and this has a number of positive consequences. First off, they feel less stressed because the situation is not a threat. They are also better able to address the challenge because they can put it into context. And they grow as they adapt and improve to deal with different situations.

Good news, as with developing a more optimistic attitude, you can retrain your brain to perceive challenges in a more positive way. Work on changing your approach, persevere and you'll not only become better at dealing with difficult situations, you'll also be more predisposed to being happy.

Change how you react to challenges

How do you react when a something bad happens? Your immediate reaction to any problem can lead you down a negative road. If you train yourself to change how you respond to and perceive problems, you can find better solutions and manage your stress levels at the same time. Jayson DeMers[xxxix] has some advice to help you shift your attitude towards problems.

Remember that problems are part of life

We encounter problems all day, every day. Some are so small that they barely register as a blip on the radar. Others are so predictable that they don't phase us. It's the problems that are a surprise or which are intense which really bother us. Remind yourself that you encounter and deal with problems all day. They are an unavoidable part of life. And remember that you are not alone. Everyone has problems, the only difference is how they deal with them.

Don't jump to conclusions.

As soon as we are faced by a problem, our brains want to jump to conclusions about the impact of that problem. If your car breaks down, you might immediately think that you are going to be late for work, that you are going to have to spend a lot of money to get it fixed, or that the kids are going to have to miss their dance classes.

Stop these voices in their tracks!

A broken down vehicle is just a broken down vehicle. Instead of jumping to conclusions, just describe the situation to yourself. "My car has broken down."

It's not easy, so start small and work your way up.

Pretend it's happening to someone else.

Remember in the section on how to train yourself to become more optimistic, you challenged your negative self-talk by asking yourself, "Would I say that to someone else?" To see challenging situations more objectively, you can try a similar trick.

Pretend that it's someone else in the situation. Your computer has just crashed! What kind of response would you have if this happened to a colleague? "Sarah's computer just crashed and she needs to call IT. Meanwhile she can access her mail and documents on her tablet."

Now you can see the situation more objectively and keep some of your heightened emotion at bay. If you can manage your emotional reaction to the situation, you can better see what you actually have control over and what the various options are for addressing it.

How bad is it really?

Once you've managed to see the situation a little more objectively, you can ask yourself how bad the consequences are really likely to be. You sent an email to the wrong person. Oops. But how serious is that really? Try listing all the possible negative outcomes that could result from your mistake. This helps you see not only the worst case scenario but the many other possible (and probably more likely) outcomes.

Choose to add a positive spin.

Try not to only react to the problem. I have a problem; now I need to fix it. Instead try to think of current or future improvements you can make. Instead of "My phone screen cracked; I need to take it for repairs," you could perhaps see the situation like this. "My phone screen cracked; this is a great opportunity to finally upgrade my handset." Keep practicing and eventually it will become more intuitive and you'll see the opportunities in each situation automatically.

Once the challenge is done and dusted, continue to control the narrative. Try to remember this experience in terms what you learned and how you benefited rather than the struggle itself. Also, think about the strength and skill that you needed to bring to bear to get past the challenge.

Learn to use stress to your advantage

Like problems, stress is an unavoidable part of life. We seem to be permanently under stress. Intense, unrelenting stress.

Stress is unhealthy when we use all our resources and don't have time to recover. We evolved the stress response to help us deal with acute stresses, but afterwards we need to rest and recover. When you feel constantly under threat, your body is operating in fight or flight mode without time to calm down and relax. That's when stress can lead to negative health and social consequences, like heart disease or divorce.

However, recent research shows that you shouldn't stress about stress. In fact you can use stress to your advantage and it can have a positive impact on your productivity and performance.

You're at the podium ready to speak to a room full of people. Your hands are sweaty. There are butterflies in your stomach. Your heart is pounding.

Just because you are feeling symptoms of stress (unpleasant as they may be), you don't need to see stress as an immediate problem. Instead of using your precious time at the podium trying desperately to calm down, you can make it work for you.

Since most of us (a resounding 91% in fact) don't deal with stress very well[xl], it's encouraging to know that there are things you can do to improve your stress reaction. Changing your stress reaction will take time though, so be patient with yourself.

Our bodies react to stress for a reason

Remember that this stress response is there for a reason. We have evolved a stress response to better equip our bodies to deal with challenging situations. So instead of being disconcerted by your jitters, remember that your body is actually freeing up energy for you to use. Embrace it.

Reach out

Ever heard people talk about how bonding a stressful experience was? This isn't just because they've worked together to overcome the odds. When you get stressed, your body actually releases oxytocin, a chemical that helps us bond with other people. Use your stress advantage to connect with others. Make your team stronger.

And make yourself stronger. Research shows that talking to others about challenges helps us to connect to the people around us, and also correlates to having more friends and close colleagues, as well as greater happiness[xli].

Learn from your experience

You've said your speech, the audience applauded, the world did not end. Lying in bed, you replay the scene over and over and over in your head. You are focused on the stressful experience instead of being happy that it's over. But that's OK, you can make it work for you. Instead of just replaying the scene, and feeling stressed about it, really analyze the situation and learn from it.

Social connections

"We are happy when we have family, we are happy when we have friends and almost all the other things we think make us happy are actually just ways of getting more family and friends."

-- Daniel Gilbert

One of the strongest recurring themes in positive psychology is the fact that people with high happiness scores have strong social connections.

In fact, social support is the greatest predictor of long-term happiness.

For example, a 2002 study at the University of Illinois[xlii] found that the happiest students studied all shared the same characteristic. They had strong connections to their friends and family and committed significant effort to spending time with them.

Various other studies have shown that:

- People report being happiest when they are with their friends[xliii].

- People who are co-operative tend to be happier[xliv].

- Sharing personal feelings with others helps relieve stress and depression[xlv].

So happy people have strong relationships. And these aren't merely superficial relationships either. Relationships that are the most beneficial are the ones where you feel comfortable sharing your feelings[xlvi].

Good relationships keep us happier and healthier

In 1938 a group of Harvard researchers wanted to find out more about what leads to a healthy and happy life. So they began an epic study. The researchers studied 258 male Harvard students with the intention of tracking them through their lives. Over time the group expanded to include the original recruits' children, and control groups were incorporated from other longitudinal studies.

The researchers studied the participants' health, relationships, life events and achievements. The participants were interviewed, their medical records examined, brain scans completed and behavior recorded.

And what did they find? Psychiatrist, Robert Waldinger, quips that the big take home message from the study is "All you need is love."

Waldinger expands on this, highlighting three lessons that they learned about relationships and health[xlvii].

1. Social connections are really good for us. The men who reported close relationships were happier, physically healthier and lived longer than their counterparts. The participants were reported being lonely suffered negative consequences for their emotional, physical and mental health.

2. The quality of relationships is key. Participants whose marriages were stable and strong benefited. While those whose marriages were fraught or high in conflict were in fact worse off than unmarried participants.

3. Strong, attached, supportive relationships protect or brains. Participants with felt they could count on their partner enjoyed better memory.

The value of relationships

Researchers have tried to put a monetary value on the benefits that social connections bring and the costs that social disconnects entail. This quantifiable measurement of happiness allows us to compare different life events to see how much impact they really have in terms of life satisfaction.

Nattavudh Powdthavee, author of the "Putting a price tag on friends, relatives and neighbors" study[xlviii] worked out values for health, a better social life, marriage, seeing friends and family regularly, divorce, unemployment, separation, and death of a spouse.

Good health provides a large amount of life satisfaction and is valued at +$463,170. A better social life works out to +$131,232. Marriage is valued at +$105,000. Meanwhile unemployment amounts to -$114,248 and death of a spouse is like losing $308,780 per year.

The study concluded that "an increase in the level of social involvements is worth up to an extra £85,000 a year [app. $131 232] in terms of life satisfaction. Actual changes in income, on the other hand, buy very little happiness."

Section 4:

Be happy by choice not chance

Is it possible to work at being happy? Experts say yes!

While your genes and your environment will affect your happiness, you can do a surprising number of small and easy things in your daily life to make you happier.

We know that DNA plays a role in hour happiness. (Studies have found that identical twins are more likely to have similar happiness scores than fraternal twins.) However, researchers think that a large portion of our happiness is determined by our daily experiences. Sonia Lyubomirsky, for example, holds that 40% of our happiness is based on our day-to-day lives[xlix].

You see, the brain is amazingly flexible. It quickly learns new things and new ways of doing things. When you practice doing things repeatedly, your brain rewires itself so that each time you do that new thing, your brain can do it more efficiently and with less conscious effort. In essence, you create a new habit. And yes, you can create a happiness habit.

Shawn Achor notes that, "Happiness is a work ethic . . . . It's something that requires our brains to train just like an athlete has to train."

From the extensive body of research into happiness, a number of practical techniques have emerged. These handy tips really will help you to become happier. Luckily, a surprising number of them don't take much time and are easy to integrate into your daily life.

The rest of this book is dedicated to the numerous techniques that the research as unearthed. While all the techniques outlined here have evidence to back them up, some are better established than others. The six that that have the most evidence are presented in detail up front. The remaining techniques have been compiled into a happiness shopping list for you to pick and choose from. Have fun!

What strategies should you choose?

In his book *Happiness Advantage*, Achor promotes a five point happiness plan focused on gratitude, journaling, performing acts of kindness, exercise and meditation[l]. He encourages people to try one of these techniques for 21 days to feel a real difference.

Richard Wiseman[li] in *59 Seconds* proposes a few techniques from the body of research that can be done in less than a minute. These include smiling more, keeping the perfect journal for a week, and performing acts of kindness.

As you decided which techniques you'd look to try, bear this in mind. Don't just select the ones that will fit neatly and easily into your daily routine. To get the most out of these techniques, you really need to make an effort[lii]. So if exercise doesn't come that easily to you, you may well benefit more from going for a walk each day than you would from meditating.

All you need is love

"Good relationships keep us happier and healthier. Period,"

-- Robert Waldinger

Many, many studies (like the long-term Harvard study discussed earlier) have shown that relationships are extremely important to happiness.

Forming and maintaining good relationships is hard work. It's not a quick fix, but has incredible long-term implications for your health and happiness. It's worth the effort.

Listen actively

Many psychologists believe that to improve your relationships so that there is a deeper connection, you can work on listening carefully to your loved ones and responding in encouraging ways.

"Active listening" means that you are listening with all senses.

Actually pay attention to what people say. (Yes, that means put down your phone or look away from your screen.) And let them say what they want to say; don't interrupt or interject with your own opinion or anecdote. Ask them questions and encourage them to share.

It's important that the person you are speaking to is aware that you are paying full attention and really listening to what they are saying. Use eye contact. Nod your head. Smile. Even saying "mmm hmmm" indicates that you are listening.

When someone knows you are really interested in what you are saying, they will feel more at ease and so communicate more easily, openly and honestly. This will help you create deeper relationships.

Here is a little experiment to try. Next time someone comes to you with a problem, be it personal or professional, put aside all distractions and give them all your attention. Encourage them to talk. Adopt open body language. Ask interested questions. (Avoid why questions that might sound judgmental.) Most important of all, don't try to provide an answer to the problem and don't pull the focus back to you by sharing your similar experiences.

Share new experiences

Studies have shown that relationships benefit from new experiences and researchers seem to have had a great deal of fun designing experiments to test whether novelty really improves relationships!

Psychologist Arthur Aron and his team set up a lab experiment to test whether couples who were asked to do a new and challenging task together, felt better about their relationships than the control group. While one control group merely walked back and forth across the room, the other couples were asked to push a ball across the room with their arms and legs tied together. The study showed that the couples who did the challenging task reported feeling more love and better satisfied with their relationships than before the task[liii].

So try new things.

For example, you could plan a trip together. Research shows that travelling with your friends or family can help strengthen relationships. These shared experiences can improve communications and improve well-being[liv].

Romantic relationship booster tips

After synthesizing the research into how to improve your romantic relationship, Richard Wiseman[lv] advises that you keep a journal for three days.

On day one, he advises that you spend 10 minutes writing down your deepest feelings about your current relationship.

On day two, he says that you should spend some time thinking about someone whose relationship is inferior to your own. Then write down three important reasons why your relationship is better than theirs.

Finally, on day three, Wiseman says that you should note down the most the quality in your partner that you value the most and explain why it is so important to you.

A few minutes of writing over three days to boost your relationship. It certainly seems with a try.

Take Action:

Here are a few other ideas to help you strengthen some of the other relationships in your life.

- Really listen and pay attention.

- Replace screen time with people time.

- Refresh a stale relationship by doing something new.

- Reach out to a family member you haven't spoken to in years.

- Call a friend when you're not OK.

- Talk about your past: your family, your childhood, your first date, your first car.

- Always show up at birthdays, anniversaries or any other special occasion.

- Leave a note saying thank you.

Gratitude

"We tend to forget that happiness doesn't come as a result of getting something we don't have, but rather of recognizing and appreciating what we do have."

-- Fredrick Koeing

Section 4: Be happy by choice not chance

It's no coincidence that self-help celebrities like Oprah Winfrey have locked onto gratitude journaling. Writing down the big and small things that you are thankful for each day, really does impact on your mood.

Numerous studies have been done into the impact of gratitude on well-being and reviews of the results show that there is an undeniable link between them[lvi].

- Gratitude will make you happier.

- It will improve your relationships[lvii].

- It can make life better for everyone around you.

- Feeling grateful will even make you feel more energized, alert, and enthusiastic[lviii].

Scientists believe that gratitude improves your happiness because you train your brain not to focus on the negative things around you but rather to see and appreciate the positive.

It's easy to take things for granted: the beautiful weather, a generous friend, a delicious meal, a roof over your head. When you actually take time to think about what you are thankful for each day, you bring these things back into mind and often re-experience the positive emotions that they created in you[lix].

Gratitude is easy to incorporate into your life, it's beneficial to you and the person you thank, and it has a positive physical and psychological benefits[lx]. Just take a few minutes each day to write down a few things that you are grateful for. Easy as that.

Keeping a gratitude journal is an excellent way to help you focus on what you appreciate in your life. While you can express your gratitude in other ways, studies indicate that the act of writing seems to be an important factor in reaping the positive benefits of gratitude.

Need some inspiration? Here are some ideas to get you started[lxi].

- Find something in nature to be grateful for.

- Say thank you to the people who love you.

- Be grateful to the people who offend you.

- Be thankful for some aspect of your body and mind.

- Identify a routine in your life to be thankful for.

Remember to be specific about what you are grateful for.

If you don't want to keep a gratitude journal, there are other ways to write down what you are thankful for. Leave a quick post-it note or send a short email thanking people for doing things for you. Or if you'd prefer to go old school write a letter!

Take Action:

- Start a gratitude journal. List a few things you are grateful for every day.

- Tell people directly that you are grateful for what they have done for you and why.

- Take someone to lunch or buy them coffee.

- Leave a quick post-it note saying thanks.

- Write a letter to someone who means a lot to you or who has done something significant for you.

- Send an email every morning to someone who's done something you appreciate.

- Relive the memory of something for which you are particularly grateful.

- Post your grateful comments on social media[lxii].

Journaling

Keeping a journal or diary can be a very powerful way to boost your mood. This is partly because the act of writing something down requires you to structure your thoughts leads you inherently to start thinking about a solution[lxiii].

Researchers have documented numerous benefits from journaling, including drastic emotional benefits and physical health benefits.

What you write about matters, and different studies indicate that journaling is more or less effective based on the topic of the writing.

Positive experience journaling

Achor advises that you describe one positive experience you had in the last day. "This is a strategy to help transform you from a task-based thinker, to a meaning based thinker who scans the world for meaning instead of endless to-dos.[lxiv]"

Negative experience journaling

Studies that asked participants to write daily journal entries detailing their deepest thoughts and feelings about a significant negative experience have found that their physical health, mood and self-esteem improved[lxv] .

Relationship venting

Writing about a break up can help you get over the failed relationship more quickly and will also help you build a stronger sense of self-identity after the break up[lxvi].

Ideal future

Although visualizing an ideal future won't make it happen, writing about it can make you happier. Participants in a study conducted by

Laura King from the Southern Methodist University who described their ideal (but not unrealistic) future for four days running were significantly happier than the control groups[lxvii].

Appreciative writing

You've already discovered the enormous benefits that practicing gratitude holds in store. You can use your journal to write down a few things each day that you are grateful for. Alternatively, you can describe what you appreciate most in your romantic partner, friend or colleague.

Affectionate writing

Writing an affectionate letter to someone you love can result in a significant increase in happiness. Studies have also found that it can lower your stress levels and even decrease your cholesterol levels![lxviii]

The perfect journal

Wiseman[lxix], having reviewed much of the research into journaling, has created a 5-day journal adopting many of the different elements that studies have shown to be effective. He's called this "the perfect journal".

Section 4: Be happy by choice not chance

This approach incorporates elements of positive journaling, gratitude, and kindness. Wiseman believes that if you keep this journal for just 5 days, you will already start to feel happier.

Day 1: List at least three things that you have been grateful for over the previous week.

Day 2: Choose an experience that you really enjoyed from your past and write about it. Imagine how you felt at the time.

Day 3: Imagine what your life would be like if you achieved all the things that are currently working for.

Day 4: Write a short letter to someone you care about explaining how much you care about them and their impact on you.

Day 5: Review the week and note three things that went really well, regardless of how trivial or momentous they were.

Take Action:

- Start writing today.

- You can write for anywhere between 2 and 20 minutes depending on what you want to write about.

- Keep a hand written journal, as this seems to be more effective than typing on a keyboard.

Exercise

"Warning: Exercise has been known to cause health and happiness."

-- Anonymous

Have you ever noticed how exercise can utterly shift your mood? Start your run grumpy and you'll end it smiling. Drag yourself to the gym in the early morning, and you'll leave full of pep. This effect has been studied by numerous researchers who have found that there is a significant link between exercise and feeling happy.

Researchers have found various links to explain this. Firstly, there is a physiological basis for why physical activity makes you feel better; exercise releases endorphins and dopamine which are the feel good chemicals of the brain[lxx]. Exercise is also often a social activity and the interactions with others can contribute to happiness[lxxi].

Various studies have also found that exercise[lxxii]:

- increases your energy,

- improves your sleep,

- helps you be more creative,

- increases your productivity,

- improves your memory,

- helps you cope with challenges in a positive way, and

- increases your overall brain performance.

An extensive Cochrane Review of studies on exercise and depression has shown that there is compelling evidence that exercise is a significant way to combat depression[lxxiii].

In light of this evidence, experts recommend exercise as a good way to improve your happiness. Achor suggests that you exercise for 10 minutes a day, arguing that this will "train your brain to believe your behavior matters, which causes a cascade of success throughout the rest of the day.[lxxiv]" Other experts encourage you to aim for at least 30 minutes a day.

Take Action:

- Exercise from 10 minutes upwards each day.

- Choose an activity that is suited to your lifestyle and fitness level.

- To get a bonus happiness boost, exercise outdoors with someone else.

Meditate and be mindful

"If you are quiet enough, you will hear the flow of the universe. You will feel its rhythm. Go with this flow. Happiness lies ahead. Meditation is the key."

-- Buddha

Many people who practice mindfulness or meditation report feeling more relaxed and better able to cope with daily stress. They experience a shift in reality. The world around them changes and becomes calmer and easier to navigate. While these experiences may sound religious or esoteric, there is also evidence to back them up.

Meditation has dozens of benefits

Psychology Today collated some of the research results relating to meditation[lxxv]. These studies show that meditation:

- improves boosts your immune system

- reduces pain (better than morphine!)

- improves cardiovascular health

- decreases inflammation

- increases positive emotion

- decreases depression

- decreases anxiety

- decreases stress

- increases social connection and emotional intelligence

- makes you more compassionate

- makes you feel less lonely

- improves your self-control

- improves your ability to introspect

- increases your focus and attention

- improves your memory

- improves decision making

- can help you overcome addiction

Shawn Achor in his discussion of the Happiness Advantage states, "It's not necessarily reality that shapes us but that the lens through which your brain views the world shapes your reality." And studies into meditation seem to bear this out.

Meditation physically affects our brains and bodies

Scientists have shown that people who practice mindfulness meditation actually have lower levels of stress hormone in their bodies after performing a stressful activity like public speaking than others who practice more conventional forms of stress management[lxxvi].

Other researchers have found that the brains of participants who took a Mindfulness-Based

Stress Reduction program for eight weeks physically changed. These changes were focused on the hippocampus, the area of the brain linked to regulating emotion, arousal, and responsiveness[lxxvii].

Researchers have even found that the relaxed state produced by meditation, yoga, and breathing exercises switches on genes that are related to augmenting our immune system, reducing inflammation, and fighting a range of conditions from arthritis to high blood pressure to diabetes.

Meditation also reduces the density of brain tissue associated with anxiety and worry, while it enhances the areas lined to mental processing and empathy.

So start meditating

There are many different kind of meditation and finding the right one for you is important as research shows that the type of meditation you choose will affect whether you stick with it or not. You need to enjoy your meditation.

But don't be intimidated if you have never meditated before. There are many videos and guides online to help you, and a quantity of relaxation and meditation apps. But you don't even need these to get started.

Take Action:

For a quick start into Mindfulness Meditation:

- Sit quietly and comfortably.

- Relax (or close) your eyes.

- Pay attention to your breathing.

- Whenever you get distracted, notice the thought or feeling and then let it go and return to the present.

- Bring your focus back to breathing.

- Start by meditating for a couple of minutes. You can extend this later.

Perform acts of kindness

"If you want happiness for an hour, take a nap. If you want happiness for a day, go fishing. If you want happiness for a year, inherit a fortune. If you want happiness for a lifetime, help somebody."

-- Chinese Proverb

It is better to give than to receive. This sentiment has been shared across the ages by different cultures and beliefs.

Now we have the evidence to back up this ancient knowledge. Brain imaging shows that giving lights up the same areas of the brain as food and sex, implying that we have evolved to give and be kind.

Research also shows that spending money on others makes you happier than spending money on yourself. Giving donations to charities or buying gifts for others can boost your happiness significantly[lxxviii].

However, giving doesn't only refer to financial transactions.

Simply acts of kindness like writing a thank you note, donating to a food drive or helping someone change a tire will also make you feel happy[lxxix].

Unfortunately there is a flip side to giving: being taking advantage of. To avoid this try to give to causes that you are passionate about. Give to effective and transparent charities. Offer your time rather than money. Volunteer - don't wait to be asked. Don't let people guilt trip you into giving[lxxx].

And, as it happens, acts of kindness are contagious. Do something kind for someone and they are likely to do something kind for someone else in return. In a sense, it's the pay it forward principle. When someone does something kind for you, you are prompted to do something kind as well.

There have been some fabulous examples in the past few years. In 2014 a Starbucks customer paid for the coffee of the next person in the queue. Instead of merely accepting this generosity, the next person paid for the person behind them, and so on for 11 hours and 378 customers[lxxxi]!

Regularly do kind things regularly other people and you'll quickly experience a happiness shift. This does not mean that you need to make large donations to charities or volunteer hours and hours of your time. A few small non-financial acts of kindness every day will do wonder•s. Compliment someone. Get in touch with an old friend.

Take Action:

Try to do a few acts of kindness every day, the possibilities are endless!

- Send an email that compliments or appreciates someone.

- Say hello to the person next to you in the elevator.

- Help someone in passing, whether it's helping a mother carry her stroller up the stairs, or supporting an elderly person across the road.

- Drive kindly – give others space to merge into the lane, smile at other drivers.

- Leave a generous tip for a waiter with a note of thanks.

Your happiness shopping list

Improving your social connections, being grateful, journaling, meditating and getting exercise are the big guns, but there are loads of other techniques that have all kinds of beneficial side effects, including happiness.

Get a dog

"A person can learn a lot from a dog ... about living each day with unbridled exuberance and joy, about seizing the moment and following your heart ... about friendship and selflessness and, above all else, unwavering loyalty."

— John Grogan

There is a body of research that indicates that dog owners are happier, more satisfied at work and more sociable than people without a dog.

Researchers have found, for example, that dog owners who have had a heart attack have better recovery than those without a dog[lxxxii].

Studies also shows that dog owners cope well with daily stress, are more relaxed, have lower blood pressure in stressful situations and have high self-esteem[lxxxiii]. Experiments have even been done that show that having your dog in the room with you when you are doing a stressful task will lower your stress response.

What exactly is it about dogs?

It might be that dogs are the best non-judgmental friends around. It could be that you experience the positive benefits of touch when you stroke or pet your dog. Even looking into your dog's large, loving eyes will boost your happiness, as it raises the oxytocin levels in your brain[lxxxiv].

Over and above all of these, walking your dog brings the benefits of exercise, being outdoors and engaging in social interaction into play:

- Dog owners are almost twice as active as non-dog owners.

- Dog owners are smiled at or approached by strangers far more often than other walkers[lxxxv].

- Dog owners take on average 2760 more steps per day than non-dog owners[lxxxvi].

- Dog owners watch less TV than non-dog owners.

- Dog owners are likely to pursue outdoor hobbies and activities.

So if you are able to own and care for a dog, consider this as a super boost to your health and happiness. Unfortunately, while there is evidence to support the impact that cats have on health, there is little evidence to show that cats have the same impact on mood.

Take Action:

- Get a dog and give it a cuddle.

- Borrow a dog and take it for walk.

- Go up to someone walking their dog and engage them in conversation.

Sleep well

We all need to sleep well. Study after study has shown that adults typically need eight hours of sleep a night and that proper sleep is essential for our well-being.

- Sleep improves memory retention and learning new tasks[lxxxvii].

- Inadequate sleep is associated with family issues, problems at school, physical health problems, and depression[lxxxviii].

- Sleep deprivation is linked to obesity and diabetes[lxxxix].

- Sleep deprivation is also associated with impairments to memory, thinking speed, reaction time, and cognitive ability[xc].

- Sleep deprivation is also linked to mood instability, over-reacting and poor judgment[xci].

To boost your mood and your well-being you need to get a good night's sleep, every night. This means that you should get approximately eight hours of uninterrupted sleep, which is harder than it sounds.

Take Action:

Here are a few tips to help improve your sleep.

- Avoid caffeine in the five or six hours before bedtime

- Establish a bedtime routine.

- Ensure that your bedroom is dark and a comfortable temperature.

- Avoid spending time looking at a screen before bed time.

- Make sure you're tired – get enough exercise during the day.

- Keep the bedroom for sleep and sex.

Get outside

A gorgeous mountain hike, a swim in a forest pool, diving a coral reef, it's common sense really: nature makes us happy (well, most of us). But did you know that a house plant can make you feel good[xcii]? Or that trees can lower the murder rate in a city[xciii]? The natural world really does improve people's well-being.

Section 4: Be happy by choice not chance

You don't need to travel to a tropical island or go on safari to reap the benefits of nature. Spend 15 minutes in your local park and you will already start to you feel psychologically restored.

There are in fact numerous benefits from spending time outdoors. First and foremost, researchers have found, in a number of studies, that getting outside makes people feel happier[xciv]. In one experiment, researchers got people to take a walk. Half the participants walked for 50 minutes in an urban setting. The other half in a natural setting[xcv]. The participants who walked out in nature experienced decreased anxiety, decreased rumination (running over things in your mind), and fewer negative emotions. They also maintained their positive attitude well and experienced improved working memory.

New technologies have allowed scientists to explore the link between space and attitude in exciting new detail. The Mappiness project[xcvi] captures in real time where people are and how they feel using a Smart phone app. Over 35 000 people have volunteered as part of the study. Researcher George MacKerron found that people are not happy at work, but are happy on vacation, with friends and listening to music. "They're also very, very happy when they are outside."[xcvii]

Additional positive mental benefits from spending time in nature include:

- Being outdoors reduces mental fatigue[xcviii], broadens your thinking, improves your creative problem solving[xcix] and improves your working memory[c].

- Being in nature decreases stress and anxiety, although the reasons for this are still largely unknown[ci].

- Mother nature encourages you to be kind and generous [cii].

- Being outdoors makes you feel more alive, even overcoming feelings of exhaustion[ciii].

Actually spending time out of doors is one thing, but researchers John Zelenski and Elizabeth Nisbet wanted to explore if how we feel about nature impacts on our happiness. Connectedness to nature is not a measure of how much time you spend in nature but rather how important being outdoors is to you, and whether you consider it an important part of yourself.

The researchers found that our emotional connectedness to nature is different from the other psychological connections in our lives, like our social or cultural connections. They also discovered that our connectedness to nature is a good predictor of happiness, regardless of other factors[civ].

Take Action:

All this gives you an excellent reason to get outside:

- Plan a weekend trip to a nature reserve.

- Spend your lunch hour in the park.

- Instead of reaching for a cup of coffee to pep you up, step outside.

- Look out the wi0ondow or load nature scenes as the wallpaper on your computer.

Enjoy the sun (in moderation)

Related to spending time outdoors, it seems a good dose of sunshine can also make us happier.

In fact, people who don't get enough sunshine can suffer from Seasonal Affective Disorder (SAD). Sometimes called "winter blues" this depressive disorder effects people when the days are shorter and there is less sunlight. It's been estimated that up to 20% of Americans are affected by Seasonal Affective Disorder (SAD) each winter[cv]. Sufferers experience low mood, low energy, irritability, difficulty concentrating, changes in eating patterns and, in some cases, more serious depression.

While the research into this area is not definitive, there are a number of theories as to why and how sunshine might make us feel happier.

- Research is emerging to show that low vitamin D levels are linked to low mood. Feeling sunshine on your skin helps your body to produce Vitamin D.

- Regular exposure to sunlight can increase your serotonin levels, making you more active and alert[cvi].Serotonin creation is triggered when sunlight hits the retina in the eyes. This is why full-spectrum light therapy works for people with SAD.

Limited-spectrum artificial light doesn't have the same effect.

- Exposure to sunlight also results in a drop in melatonin, the chemical that our bodies produce to get us into a calm and relaxed state, ready for sleep. Too much melatonin might cause you to feel lethargic[cvii].

- Recent research has also posited a link between mood and the number of sunny hours in the day (regardless of the weather or pollution levels)[cviii]. The more sunny hours, the happier everyone feels.

There are additional benefits to getting sufficient sun. Studies have shown that as well as boosting your mood, sunshine (specifically vitamin D) may help prevent certain cancers[cix]. And it is an important component of your sleep cycle; each morning your cycle restarts with the sunrise[cx]. UV exposure also releases nitric oxide which lowers blood pressure[cxi].

Advice to enjoy the sun does, of course, need to be tempered by warnings to avoid the sun since, as we all know, too much sun has been linked to skin cancer. In fact, it's possible that sunscreen may be playing a role in the lower Vitamin D levels that doctors are finding. A more indoor lifestyle is probably also playing a role. So get out and enjoy the sun, in moderation.

Take Action:

- Take a 15 to 20 walk in the early morning sunshine without your sunscreen (when the chance of getting sunburned is low).

- Use your coffee and lunch breaks to have a sun break.

- Have your vitamin D levels tested, and if necessary get Vitamin D supplements.

- During dark, winter months if you feel the winter blues, use a full spectrum light box for 30 minutes a day.

Buy experiences not stuff

"If more of us valued food and cheer and song above hoarded gold, it would be a merrier world."

— J.R.R. Tolkien

Section 4: Be happy by choice not chance

Can money buy happiness? The answer to this isn't actually as simple as you might think. Conventional wisdom says no, money can't buy happiness but a surprisingly large number of people still think that when they are rich (or richer) they will be happy[cxii].

Finding the rather complex answer to the money-happiness question started with research conducted in the late-1970s which concluded that money doesn't lead to happiness. Researchers studied lottery winners against other randomly-selected people[cxiii]. They found that there was no significant difference between the happiness levels of the two groups. Winning the Lottery didn't make people happier. The only real difference was that the people in the control group got more joy out of the small things in life.

Not only does an unexpected bonus not make you happy, even when people have obtained their wealth through their own effort, there still appears to be no link between money and happiness. It seems that when you get a salary increase or buy a new car, you only feel a short-lived burst of happiness. After a while the feeling passes and your new house or beautiful jewelry just becomes part of the status quo.

What's more, studies exploring materialism and happiness have shown that people who value possessions are likely to be less happy and less satisfied[cxiv].

More recently, we've learn that money can buy happiness, up to a point. Researchers Kahneman and Deaton studied the happiness levels in families with varied incomes. They found that additional money in a family income below $75 000 does increase happiness. However, above this threshold the link between money and happiness ceases[cxv].

This is borne out at the country level. Poor countries (those with a low GDP) are typically less happy, but after a certain point, wealth is no longer a predictor of happiness.

To complicate this question even further, there actually are some things that you can spend money on that will increase your happiness.

1. Spend money on other people. Studies have consistently shown that people who send a higher percentage of their income on other people are happier than people who send their money on themselves[cxvi].

2. Spend money to free up your own time. Researchers found that people who spend money to get others to do chores that they do not enjoy, thus freeing up their own time, feel more positive than those who don't[cxvii].

The relationship between money and happiness can be summarized as follows. Money helps us become happier when it helps us meet our basic needs. Beyond that, money doesn't make us happy. More specifically, spending money on possessions does not make us happy. But spending money on experiences and other people does make us happier.

So go on holiday. Take a trip to the theatre. Go skydiving. Having new and interesting experiences will boost your happiness, especially if you share the experience with others (during and after).

What's more, give your loved one's experiences as gifts, and you'll spread the happiness around.

Take Action:

- Instead of saving up to buy yourself a luxury treat, decide to rather save up for an experience.

- Next time you give a birthday present, give an experience (a shared meal, a movie, learning how to kite surf, teaching someone how to make a much-loved dish).

Smile

"Sometimes your joy is the source of your smile, but sometimes your smile can be the source of your joy."

— Thich Nhat Hanh

People smile when they are happy, but did you know that you can become happy because you are smiling?

Some rather odd experiments in the early 80's have shown that people who force their muscles into a smile (by holding a pencil between their teeth or saying "eeeee") start to feel happier[cxviii].

Section 4: Be happy by choice not chance

The fact that these smiles aren't genuine doesn't seem to matter very much.

While the mechanism behind this effect is still not fully understood, there is one theory that smiling constricts veins in the face that would ultimately lead to a reduction in the amount of blood from the carotid artery to the brain.

However it happens, the effect seems to be real and we can exploit this interesting fact of biology to our own benefit.

This is probably the easiest technique to fit into your everyday routine. Just smile more. You don't even need to be smiling at someone or something. The simple act of pulling your facial muscles into a smile configuration will help you become happier.

Do try to make the smile as genuine as possible. Maybe think of something funny or endearing as you fake smile your way up the elevator. Also try to maintain the smile for 30 seconds if you can.

As you fake a smile to make yourself happier, you could well make someone else happier too. When you smile at someone, they will smile back[cxix]. It's instinctive and unthinking. So you can use your smile to change your own mood, and make the world around you a happier place.

Take Action:

It's quite easy to forget to smile on purpose. So here are some ways to remind yourself.

- Smile at yourself whenever you look in a mirror.

- Associate something with smiling, like a color or word, and smile each time you see or hear it.

- Watch funny YouTube videos.

- Think of a happy memory.

- And if you're desperate, put a pencil between your teeth!

Straighten your posture

Believe it or not, good posture will affect your mood and your performance!

Get students to sit up straight when they do a math test and you'll find that they do better and feel happier than their slouching counterparts.

At least the students in the study conducted by researchers at Colorado Collage did[cxx].

Not only that, good posture can increase your energy levels, improve your confidence and reduce your fears[cxxi]. People even report that it is harder to remember negative memories when they stand or sit up tall.

How is this possible? Basically, the effect is psychological. When we're sad or miserable, we tend to lower our heads and slouch our backs. So we can basically trick our brains into feeling positive by adopting a tall, straight posture with chest out and chin up.

Good posture can improve your mood, so channel your mother's voice in the back of your head and stop slouching.

Take Action:

You can also try a few creative tricks to remind you[cxxii].

- Stand against a wall with your head, shoulders and butt just touching the wall. This is what good posture feels like!

- Stick a post-it to your computer screen, reminding you to sit up.

- Associate a color with posture. Each time you see that color, sit up!

- Stand up straight. Get someone to put tape across your back from your left shoulder to your right hip, and from your right shoulder to your left hip. You'll feel the tape move if you start to slouch.

- Strengthen your core muscles doing stomach and back exercises.

- Put a photo or picture just higher than head height on the wall behind your desk so you have to look up to see it.

- Adjust your driving mirror so it's a bit higher so you have to sit taller while you drive.

Take the good with the bad

It sounds rather counter intuitive but feeling mixed emotions together is another proven way to boost positivity. By now it's fairly well-understood accepted that we should express our emotions, both negative and positive. (Though doesn't appear to be practiced as widely as it should be.) But feeling positive and negative emotions and expressing them at the same time?

A number of studies[cxxiii] have looked at the impact it has on participants when they acknowledge the complexity of life and embrace a wide range of emotions, good and bad. These studies show that mixed-emotional experiences improve well-being.

So when something bad happens, recognize your negative feelings but also try to see the bright side. This may take the sting out of negative experiences in the moment and can also have a lasting effect.

As a bonus, feeling negative and positive emotions together has also been found to improve health, specifically can reduce typical age-related decline[cxxiv].

Take Action:

- Don't suppress your negative feelings. Acknowledge them and then actively seek a positive angle.

- When you journal about a negative experience, also think about any positive outcomes.

Keep your happy friends close

Research has shown that happiness is contagious. If you are surrounded by happy people you are more likely to be happy yourself.

A longitudinal study undertaken in Framingham, Massachusetts over three generations has shown that happiness moves through a population[cxxv]. In fact happiness is so contagious that it can even affect the friend of a friend of a friend.

This impact is even stronger if you are geographically close to your happy friends. Friends who live within a mile of you have a massive impact on your happiness (but not your level of sadness). Neighbors and family also effect on your happiness but not to the same degree.

Take Action:

- Engage with your happy friends and neighbors.

- Create connections with new people in your immediate community.

Learn something new

Earlier, you read that happiness improves learning because it activates a center of the brain called the *nucleus accumbens*. When you are feeling positive emotions, your brain makes itself open to new experiences, and becomes better at retaining and analyzing information.

You can use this process to boost your happiness, your self-confidence, and your resilience by learning something new. A new challenge will also help you stay curious and engaged.

Learning a new skill may bring more stress in the short-term but will contribute to a greater daily sense of happiness later on[cxxvi]. Researchers suggest that you can reduce the short-term stress by making sure that you choose what you want to learn (sense of autonomy) and do the activity with others if you can (social connectedness).

You don't have to achieve your ultimate goal to see the benefits and you don't need to engage in formal learning. Taking up a hobby, joining a club, or learning to play a sport will all bring you happiness as your brain revels in the novelty.

Take Action:

- Choose something you've always wanted to do and learn how to do it.

- Can you learn this with someone?

Give up one of your favorite things

It sounds rather odd, but if you give up one of your favorite things for a few days it will actually increase your willpower and boost your happiness.

Think about it for a few seconds. When you've denied yourself chocolate for a few days, what do you do when you next have some? You don't scoff it down unthinkingly, you savor it. And that's the trick.

In a world of abundance, many of us are able to fulfil our wants and needs at virtually any time. We aren't often denied what we want. Denying ourselves the odd daily pleasure is a great way to ensure that we don't take that treat for granted but that we savor it instead.

Section 4: Be happy by choice not chance

Religious groups and philosophers have long advocated for self-denial, whether it's a monthly fast for Muslims during Ramadan, the ascetic life of a Buddhist or the self-denial of Jesuit monks.

By denying yourself something small for a few days, you are exercising your self-control. A skill which can stead you in good stead when it comes to happiness.

What's more, researchers have also shown that if you feel that the time you have available to share with others is limited, you will appreciate that time more[cxxvii].

Take Action:

- Identify something that you really enjoy and give it up for a couple of days. Coffee is an easy example. When you next have a cup of coffee, you'll be more aware of the taste and will enjoy the experience that much more.

- Be conscious of how much time is left when you're on holiday or at an event. We often count down the days to the start of a holiday. Try counting down the days left in the holiday.

Put down your phone

It sounds a bit reactionary to say "put down your phone, it's making you unhappy," -- teenagers would certainly say so -- but there is evidence that links frequent cell phone use and reduced happiness.

Researchers at Kent State University have been exploring the links between cell phone use and various happiness-related factors. Their studies have shown that, "high frequency cell phone users tended to have lower grade point averages (GPA), higher anxiety, and lower satisfaction with life (happiness) relative to their peers who used the cell phone less often."[cxxviii]

They have also found links between cell phone use and feeling emotionally close to friends and relatives. While female participants in the study were able to feel closer to friends and family by calling or texting them, male participants experienced no improvement. Both male and female students who used cell phones compulsively or at inappropriate times felt less socially connected to parents and peers[cxxix]. This study seems to show that it's not just how much people use their phones that matters, but how and when as well.

The causal link between cell phone use and happiness is not clear. It may well be that high cell phone use correlates with less time outside and less exposure to sunshine[cxxx]. There also seems to be a link between frequent cell phone use and how much exercise people do[cxxxi]. Or it may be that frequent cell phone checkers are already unhappy and are trying to improve how they feel.

Psychologist, David Strayer, has researched people's cell-phone behavior as they drive and has found that when they use a phone, what they notice is cut in half."[cxxxii] This has obviously implications when you are driving, but can also impact on your social interactions and your engagement with your environment.

Since we know that being outdoors, enjoying the sunshine, getting exercise and having quality interpersonal relationships are all linked to happiness, it follows that if frequent or inappropriate cell phone use affects these we should take this seriously.

More research needs to be done into this area before any definitive statements can be made about cell phones and happiness, (and shouldn't it be what we're doing on the cell phone, rather than the device itself?) In the meantime, there are a few things you can try.

Take Action:

- Pay attention to how much time you spend on your cellphone and what you use it for. Does your cell phone interfere with your interactions with other people? Does your cell phone interfere with your enjoyment of outdoor activities?

- Do an experiment. Give yourself a few hours (or even a day!) without your phone and see how you feel afterwards.

Conclusion

Thank you again for downloading this book!

I hope this book was able to help you to develop your happiness skills and so enable you to embrace a more positive attitude. This in turn should help you achieve success.

You've now got a long list of strategies to try out as you seek to make your life happier and more successful.

If you're tempted to pursue happiness relentlessly with your full focus, don't. If you pressurize yourself to be happy, chances are you are not going to meet your own expectations. By all means adopt the attitudes and behaviors that research has linked to happiness, but do so in a relaxed and fun way[cxxxiii].

The next step after finishing this book is to take what you have learned and put it into action.

Happiness Advantage

Choose which happiness strategies you want to employ. Rope in a friend or family member to start some happiness training with you. Enjoy the journey and have fun as you go!

Thank you and good luck!

Endnotes

[i] Shawn Achor, "The happy secret to better work" *TedX* May 2011, accessed at https://www.ted.com/talks/shawn_achor_the_happy_secret_to_better_work#t-715518 on 5 Dec 2017

[ii] Barbara Fredrickson *Positivity* Three Rivers Press, 2009

[iii] Fredrickson, B.L., (2001). The role of positive emotions in positive psychology: The broaden-and-build theory of positive emotions. American Psychologist, 56, 218-226

[iv] Manfred Spitzer (2011) "Learning Brings Happiness" accessed at https://www.humboldt-foundation.de/web/kosmos-cover-story-97-3.html on 7 Dec 2017

[v] www.pursuitofhappiness.org

[vi] Patrick Allan 14 Sept 2015 "What Research Says Happiness Really Is" *LifeHacker* accessed at https://lifehacker.com/what-research-says-happiness-really-is-1730503184 on 7 Dec 2017

[vii] Shawn Achor "You Have to See Your Happiness to Believe It" *Success Magazine* accessed at http://goodthinkinc.com/success-magazine-you-have-to-see-your-happiness-to-believe-it/on 8 Dec 2017

[viii] Lyubomirsky S, King L, Diener E. "The benefits of frequent positive affect: does happiness lead to success?" Psychology Bulletin " 2005 Nov;131(6):803-55.

[ix] Manfred Spitzer "Learning Brings Happiness" accessed at https://www.humboldt-foundation.de/web/kosmos-cover-story-97-3.html on 8 Dec 2017

[x] Lyubomirsky S, King L, Diener E. "The benefits of frequent positive affect: does happiness lead to success?" Psychology Bulletin " 2005 Nov;131(6):803-55.

xi Manfred Spitzer "Learning Brings Happiness" accessed at https://www.humboldt-foundation.de/web/kosmos-cover-story-97-3.html on 8 Dec 2017

xii Andrew J. Oswald, Eugenio Proto, and Daniel Sgroi, "Happiness and Productivity," Journal of Labor Economics 33, no. 4 (October 2015): 789-822. https://doi.org/10.1086/681096

xiii Martin Seligman *Authentic Happiness* Simon and Schuster, 2002

xiv D. G. Myers, in The Pursuit of Happiness, HarperCollins, 1993

xv Thomas A. Wright and Russell Cropanzano "Well-being, satisfaction and job performance: another look at the happy/productive worker thesis." *Academy of Management Proceedings* Aug 1997 doi: 10.5465/AMBPP.1997.4988986

xvi Rebecca Alber "How Are Happiness and Learning Connected?" 4 March 2013 accessed at https://www.edutopia.org/blog/happiness-learning-connection-rebecca-alber on 8 Dec 2017

xvii Manfred Spitzer "Learning Brings Happiness" accessed at https://www.humboldt-foundation.de/web/kosmos-cover-story-97-3.html on 8 Dec 2017

xviii "Creativity" *This Emotional Life* accessed at http://thisemotionallife.org/topic/creativity/creativity on 8 Dec 2017

xix Daisy Coyle, RD "How Being Happy Makes You Healthier" HealthLine 27 August 2017 accessed at https://www.healthline.com/nutrition/happiness-and-health#section3 on 8 Dec 2017

xx Sapranaviciute-Zabazlajeva, L., Luksiene, D., Virviciute, D., Bobak, M., & Tamosiunas, A. (2017). Link between healthy lifestyle and psychological well-being in Lithuanian adults aged 45–72: a cross-sectional study. BMJ Open, 7(4), e014240. http://doi.org/10.1136/bmjopen-2016-014240

xxi Sapranaviciute-Zabazlajeva, L., Luksiene, D., Virviciute, D., Bobak, M., & Tamosiunas, A. (2017). Link between healthy lifestyle and psychological well-being in Lithuanian adults aged 45–72: a cross-sectional study. BMJ Open, 7(4), e014240. http://doi.org/10.1136/bmjopen-2016-014240

xxii Steptoe A, O'Donnell K, Marmot M, Wardle J. "Positive affect, psychological well-being, and good sleep." Journal of Psychosomatic Research. 2008 Apr;64(4):409-15. doi: 10.1016/j.jpsychores.2007.11.008.

xxiii Cohen S, Alper CM, Doyle WJ, Treanor JJ, Turner RB. "Positive emotional style predicts resistance to illness after experimental exposure to rhinovirus or influenza a virus." Psychosomatic Medicine 2006 Nov-Dec;68(6):809-15. Epub 2006 Nov 13. DOI: 10.1097/01.psy.0000245867.92364.3c

xxiv Steptoe, A., Wardle, J., & Marmot, M. (2005). Positive affect and health-related neuroendocrine, cardiovascular, and inflammatory processes. Proceedings of the National Academy of Sciences of the United States of America, 102(18), 6508–6512. http://doi.org/10.1073/pnas.0409174102

xxv Steptoe A1, Wardle J. "Positive affect and biological function in everyday life" Neurobiology of Aging. 2005 Dec;26 Suppl 1:108-12. Epub 2005 Oct 6.

xxvi Zautra, A. J., Johnson, L. M., & Davis, M. C. (2005). Positive Affect as a Source of Resilience for Women in Chronic Pain. Journal of Consulting and Clinical Psychology, 73(2), 212–220. http://doi.org/10.1037/0022-006X.73.2.212

xxvii Berges, I.-M., Seale, G., & Ostir, G. V. (2011). Positive Affect and Pain Ratings in Persons with Stroke. Rehabilitation Psychology, 56(1), 52–57. http://doi.org/10.1037/a0022683

xxviii Lawrence, E. M., Rogers, R. G., & Wadsworth, T. (2015). Happiness and Longevity in the United States. Social Science & Medicine (1982), 145, 115–119. http://doi.org/10.1016/j.socscimed.2015.09.020

xxix Eric S. Kim, Nansook Park, Christopher Peterson "Dispositional Optimism Protects Older Adults From Stroke" *Stroke* October 2011 DOI: 10.1161/STROKEAHA.111.613448

xxx PS Fry, DL Debats "Perfectionism and the five-factor personality traits as predictors of mortality in older adults." *Journal of Health Psychology* 2009 May;14(4):513-24. DOI: 10.1177/1359105309103571

xxxi Lyubomirsky S1, Dickerhoof R, Boehm JK, Sheldon KM. "Becoming happier takes both a will and a proper way: An experimental longitudinal intervention to boost well-being." Emotion, Vol 11(2), Apr 2011, 391-402. DOI: 10.1037/a0022575

xxxii Brunwasser SM1, Gillham JE, Kim ES. "A meta-analytic review of the Penn Resiliency Program's effect on depressive symptoms" J Consult Clin Psychol. 2009 Dec;77(6):1042-54. DOI: 10.1037/a0017671.

xxxiii "The benefits of optimism" *The Positive Psychlopedia* accessed at https://positivepsychlopedia.com/year-of-happy/the-benefits-of-optimism/ on 8 Dec 2017

xxxiv Tindle HA1 Chang YF, Kuller LH, Manson JE, Robinson JG, Rosal MC, Siegle GJ, Matthews KA. "Optimism, cynical hostility, and incident coronary heart disease and mortality in the Women's Health Initiative."

Circulation. 2009 Aug 25;120(8):656-62. doi: 10.1161/CIRCULATIONAHA.108.827642.

xxxv P. Kamen, Leslie & E. P. Seligman, Martin. (1987). Explanatory style and health. Current Psychology: Research and Reviews. 6. 207-218. 10.1007/BF02686648.

xxxvi Varda Liberman, Nicholas R Anderson, Lee Ross "Achieving difficult agreements: Effects of Positive Expectations on negotiation processes and outcomes" Journal of Experimental Social Psychology Volume 46, Issue 3, May 2010, Pages 494-504 doi.org/10.1016/j.jesp.2009.12.010

xxxvii Wiseman, Richard. 59 Seconds: Think A Little, Change A Lot (p. 339). Pan Macmillan. Kindle Edition.

xxxviii Martin Seligman *Learned Optimism* Knopf Doubleday Publishing Group 1990

xxxix Jayson DeMers "How to Change Your Mindset to See Problems as Opportunities" accessed at https://www.inc.com/jayson-demers/how-to-change-your-mindset-to-see-problems-as-opportunities.html on 6 Dec 2017

xl Michelle Gielan "You Can Improve Your Default Response to Stress" Harvard Business Review January 5, 2017 Acxcessed at http://goodthinkinc.com/hbr-you-can-improve-your-default-response-to-stress/ on 6 Dec 2017

xli Keaton Brown and Roya Taghehchian, (2016) "Bottled Up: An Experiential Intervention for Emotional Suppression" *Journal of Family Psychotherapy* Volume 27, 2016 - Issue 4

xlii Ed Diener and Martin Seligman

xliii Larson, Mannell, & Zuzanek, 1986

xliv Lu & Argyle, 1991

[xlv] Jackson, Soderlind & Weiss, 2000, Horesh, Apter, 2006

[xlvi] Jackson, Soderlind & Weiss, 2000, Horesh, Apter, 2006

[xlvii] Robert Waldinger "What makes a good life? Lessons from the longest study on happiness" *TedX* accessed at https://www.ted.com/talks/robert_waldinger_what_mak es_a_good_life_lessons_from_the_longest_study_on_ha ppiness on 7 Dec 2017

[xlviii] Nattavudh Powdthavee "Putting a price tag on friends, relatives, and neighbours: Using surveys of life satisfaction to value social relationships" *The Journal of Socio-Economics* Volume 37, Issue 4, August 2008, Pages 1459-1480 https://doi.org/10.1016/j.socec.2007.04.004

[xlix] Sonja Lyubomirsky Kennon M. Sheldon David Schkade (2005) "Pursuing Happiness: The Architecture of Sustainable Change" *Review of General Psychology* 2005, Vol. 9, No. 2, 111–131 DOI: 10.1037/1089-2680.9.2.111

[l] Shawn Achor *The Happiness Advantage: The Seven Principles of Positive Psychology That Fuel Success and Performance at Work* Crown Publishing Group, 2010

[li] Wiseman, Richard. 59 Seconds: Think A Little, Change A Lot (p. 339). Pan Macmillan. Kindle Edition.

[lii] KM Sheldon, S Lyubomirsky (2007) "Is it possible to become happier? (And if so, how?)" *Social and Personality Psychology Compass*, 1, pp 129-145

[liii] Aron A, Norman CC, Aron EN, McKenna C, Heyman RE. "Couples' shared participation in novel and arousing activities and experienced relationship quality." Journal of Personality and Social Psychology 2000 Feb;78(2):273-84.

[liv] Durko, Angela M. and Petrick, James F., "The Benefits of Travel: : Family and Relationships Review of Literature" (2016). Tourism Travel and Research Association: Advancing Tourism Research Globally. 16.

[lv] Wiseman, Richard. 59 Seconds: Think A Little, Change A Lot (p. 350). Pan Macmillan. Kindle Edition.

[lvi] Wood AM, Froh JJ, Geraghty AW. "Gratitude and well-being: a review and theoretical integration." *Clinical Psychology Review* 2010 Nov;30(7):890-905. DOI: 10.1016/j.cpr.2010.03.005

[lvii] Sara B. Algoe, Shelly L. Gable, and Natalya C. Maisel "It's the little things: Everyday gratitude as a booster shot for romantic relationships" *Personal Relationships*, 17 (2010), 217–233.

[lviii] McCullough, Emmons, & Tsang, 2002

[lix] Ryan M. Niemiec 25 Nov 2015 "4 New and Helpful Insights on Gratitude" Psychology Today accessed at https://www.psychologytoday.com/blog/what-matters-most/201511/4-new-and-helpful-insights-gratitude on 7 Dec 2017

[lx] Ryan M. Niemiec 25 Nov 2015 "4 New and Helpful Insights on Gratitude" *Psychology Today* accessed at https://www.psychologytoday.com/blog/what-matters-most/201511/4-new-and-helpful-insights-gratitude on 7 Dec 2017

[lxi] Ryan M. Niemiec 22 Nov 2017 "Five "Thank Yous" to Say Each Day" *Psychology Today* accessed at https://www.psychologytoday.com/blog/what-matters-most/201711/five-thank-yous-say-each-day on 7 Dec 2017

[lxii] Jesus Jimenez 19 January 2017 "Top of Mind: 6 Sincere Ways to Express Gratitude" *SUCCESS Magazine* Accessed at https://www.success.com/article/top-of-mind-6-sincere-ways-to-express-gratitude on 7 Dec 2017

[lxiii] S Spera, E Buhrfeind, JW Pennebaker "Expressive writing and coping with loss" Academy of Management Journal, 1994, 3 pp 722-733

[lxiv] S Achor, Psychology Today xxxx, 23 Aug 2011, https://www.psychologytoday.com/blog/the-happiness-advantage/201108/5-ways-turn-happiness-advantage retrieved 5 Dec 2017

[lxv] S. J. Lepore and J. M. Smyth (eds). The Writing Cure: How Expressive Writing Promotes Health and Emotional Well-Being. Washington, DC: American Psychological Association.

[lxvi] Grace M. Larson, David A. Sbarra "Participating in Research on Romantic Breakups Promotes Emotional Recovery via Changes in Self-Concept Clarity" *Social Psychological and Personality Science* Volume: 6 issue: 4, page(s): 399-406 https://doi.org/10.1177/1948550614563085

[lxvii] L. A. King (2001). 'The Health Benefits of Writing About Life Goals'. Personality and Social Psychology Bulletin, 27, pages 798–807. .

[lxviii] K. Floyd, A. C. Mikkelson, C. Hesse and P. M. Pauley (2007). 'Affectionate Writing Reduces Total Cholesterol: Two Randomized, Controlled Trials'. Human Communication Research, 33, pages 119–42.

[lxix] Wiseman, Richard. 59 Seconds: Think A Little, Change A Lot (p. 349). Pan Macmillan. Kindle Edition.

[lxx] Fox KR, "The influence of physical activity on mental well-being." Public Health Nutr. 1999 Sep;2(3A):411-8.

[lxxi] Stubbe JH, de Moor MH, Boomsma DI, de Geus EJ. "The association between exercise participation and well-being: a co-twin study" Preventative Medicine 2007 Feb;44(2):148-52. Epub 2006 Oct 23.

[lxxii] "16 ways Exercise Makes You a Happier Person" accessed at https://i1.wp.com/www.pursuit-of-happiness.org/wp-

content/uploads/16ways_infographic.png?w=1500 on 6
Dec 2017

lxxiii Cooney GM, Dwan K, Greig CA, Lawlor DA, Rimer J,
Waugh FR, McMurdo M, Mead GE "Exercise for
Depression" *Cochrane Review* 12 September 2013

lxxiv As quoted in "5 Ways to Turn Happiness Into An
Advantage" Psychology Today accessed at
https://www.psychologytoday.com/blog/the-happiness-
advantage/201108/5-ways-turn-happiness-advantage on
8 Dec 2017

lxxv Emma M. Seppälä "20 Scientific Reasons to Start
Meditating Today" *Psychology Today* 11 Sept 2013
accessed at
https://www.psychologytoday.com/blog/feeling-
it/201309/20-scientific-reasons-start-meditating-today
accessed on 5 Dec 2017

lxxvi Elizabeth A, Eric Bui, Sophie A. Palitz, Noah R.
Schwarz, Maryann E. Owens, Jennifer M. Johnston, Mark
H. Pollack, Naomi M. Simon "The Effect of Mindfulness
Meditation Training on Biological Acute Stress Responses
in Generalized Anxiety Disorder" *Psychiatry Research*,
January 2017, DOI:
http://dx.doi.org/10.1016/j.psychres.2017.01.006

lxxvii Holzel, B.K., Carmody J, Vangel M, et al (2011).
"Mindfulness practice leads to increases in regional brain
gray matter density." Psychiatry Research: Neuroimaging
191(1):36-43

lxxviii E. W. Dunn, L. Aknin and M. I. Norton (2008).
'Spending Money on Others Promotes Happiness'. Science,
319, pages 1687–88.

lxxix S. Lyubomirsky, K. M. Sheldon and D. Schkade (2005).
'Pursuing Happiness: The Architecture of Sustainable
Change'. Review of General Psychology, 9, pages 111–31

[lxxx] Jenni Santil, "The Secret to Happiness is Helping Others" http://time.com/collection/guide-to-happiness/4070299/secret-to-happiness/# accessed on 5 Dec 2017

[lxxxi] Amy Blankson, 14 February 2017, "Start a Ripple of Kindness in Your Community" *Live Happy Magazine,* accessed at http://goodthinkinc.com/live-happy-start-a-ripple-of-kindness-in-your-community/ on 7 Dec 2017

[lxxxii] E. Friedmann and S. A. Thomas (1995). 'Pet Ownership, Social Support, and One-Year Survival After Acute Myocardial Infarction in the Cardiac Arrhythmia Suppression Trial (CAST)'. American Journal of Cardiology, 76, pages 1213–17. 163 D. L. Wells (2007). 'Domestic Dogs and Human

[lxxxiii] D. L. Wells (2007). 'Domestic Dogs and Human Health: An Overview'. British Journal of Health Psychology, 12, pages 145–56.

[lxxxiv] Nagasawa M1, Kikusui T, Onaka T, Ohta M."Dog's gaze at its owner increases owner's urinary oxytocin during social interaction" Horm Behav. 2009 Mar;55(3):434-41. doi: 10.1016/j.yhbeh.2008.12.002. Epub 2008 Dec 14.

[lxxxv] D. L. Wells (2004). 'The Facilitation of Social Interactions by Domestic Dogs'. Anthrozoos, 17 (4), pages 340–352.

[lxxxvi] Philippa Margaret DallEmail author, Sarah Lesley Helen Ellis, Brian Martin Ellis, P Margaret Grant, Alison Colyer, Nancy Renee Gee, Malcolm Howard Granat and Daniel Simon Mills "The influence of dog ownership on objective measures of free-living physical activity and sedentary behaviour in community-dwelling older adults: a longitudinal case-controlled study" *BMC Public Health* 9 June 2017 https://doi.org/10.1186/s12889-017-4422-5

[lxxxvii] Harms, 2013

[lxxxviii] Smaldone et al. from 2007

[lxxxix] Copinschi, 2005

[xc] Killgore, 2010

[xci] Motomura et al., 2013

[xcii] Nieuwenhuis, M., Knight, C., Postmes, T., & Haslam, S. A. (2014). The relative benefits of green versus lean office space: Three field experiments. Journal of Experimental Psychology: Applied, 20(3), 199-214. http://dx.doi.org/10.1037/xap0000024

[xciii] Kuo, F.E., & Sullivan, W.C. (2001). "Environment and crime in the inner city: Does vegetation reduce crime?" Environment and Behavior, 33(3), 343-367.

[xciv] Marc G. Berman, Ethan Kross, Katherine M. Krpan, Mary K. Askren, Aleah Burson, Patricia J. Deldin, Stephen Kaplan, Lindsey Sherdell, Ian H. Gotlib, and John Jonides "Interacting with Nature Improves Cognition and Affect for Individuals with Depression" J Affect Disorders 2012 Nov; 140(3): 300–305.

[xcv] Gregory N.Bratman Gretchen C.Daily Benjamin J.Levy James J.Gross "The benefits of nature experience: Improved affect and cognition" Landscape and Urban Planning Volume 138, June 2015, Pages 41-50

[xcvi] George MacKerron "Mapping Happiness across Space and Time" TedX accessed at https://www.youtube.com/watch?v=dvMYhjuFtt0 on 8 Dec 2017

[xcvii] Simon Worrall "We Are Wired To Be Outside" National Geographic 12 Feb 2017 Accessed at https://news.nationalgeographic.com/2017/02/nature-fix-brain-happy-florence-williams/ on 8 Dec 2017

[xcviii] Marc G. Berman, John Jonides, Stephen Kaplan "The Cognitive Benefits of Interacting With Nature"

Psychological Science Volume: 19 issue: 12, page(s): 1207-1212

[xcix] Atchley RA, Strayer DL, Atchley P (2012) Creativity in the Wild: Improving Creative Reasoning through Immersion in Natural Settings. PLoS ONE 7(12): e51474. https://doi.org/10.1371/journal.pone.0051474

[c] Marc G. Berman, Ethan Kross, Katherine M. Krpan, Mary K. Askren, Aleah Burson, Patricia J. Deldin, Stephen Kaplan, Lindsey Sherdell, Ian H. Gotlib, and John Jonides "Interacting with Nature Improves Cognition and Affect for Individuals with Depression" *J Affect Disorders* 2012 Nov; 140(3): 300–305.

[ci] Liisa Tyrväinen Ann Ojala Kalevi Korpela Timo Lanki Yuko Tsunetsugu Takahide Kagawa "The influence of urban green environments on stress relief measures: A field experiment" *Journal of Environmental Psychology* Volume 38, June 2014, Pages 1-9 https://doi.org/10.1016/j.jenvp.2013.12.005

[cii] Jia Wei Zhang Paul K. Piff Ravi Iyer Spassena Koleva Dacher Keltner "An occasion for unselfing: Beautiful nature leads to prosociality" *Journal of Environmental Psychology* Volume 37, March 2014, Pages 61-72

[ciii] Richard M.Ryan Netta Weinstein Jessey Bernstein Kirk Warren Brown Louis Mistretta Marylène Gagné "Vitalizing effects of being outdoors and in nature" *Journal of Environmental Psychology* Volume 30, Issue 2, June 2010, Pages 159-168

[civ] Zelenski, J. M., & Nisbet, E. K. (2014). Happiness and Feeling Connected The Distinct Role of Nature Relatedness. Environment and Behavior, 46(1), 3-23

[cv] "Seasonal Affective Disorder" *Psychology Today* accessed at

https://www.psychologytoday.com/conditions/seasonal-affective-disorder on 8 Dec 2017

cvi Simon N. Young "How to increase serotonin in the human brain without drugs" Journal of Psychiatry and Neuroscience 2007 Nov; 32(6): 394–399.

cvii "Seasonal Affective Disorder" *Psychology Today* accessed at https://www.psychologytoday.com/conditions/seasonal-affective-disorder on 8 Dec 2017

cviii Beecher ME, Eggett D, Erekson D, Rees LB, Bingham J, Bailey RJ, et al. Sunshine on my shoulders: Weather, pollution, and emotional distress. Journal of Affective Disorders. 2016.

cix "Vitamin D and Cancer Prevention" *National Cancer Institute* accessed at https://www.cancer.gov/about-cancer/causes-prevention/risk/diet/vitamin-d-fact-sheet#q3 on 8 Dec 2017

cx "Circadian Rhythms" National Institute of General Medical Studies accessed at https://www.nigms.nih.gov/Pages/default.aspx on 8 Dec 2017

cxi "Here comes the sun to lower your blood pressure" University of Southampton, 20 January 2014 accessed at https://www.southampton.ac.uk/news/2014/01/20-the-sun-to-lower-your-blood-pressure.page on 8 Dec 2017

cxii Wiseman, Richard. 59 Seconds: Think A Little, Change A Lot (p. 331). Pan Macmillan. Kindle Edition.

cxiii P. Brickman, D. Coates and R. Janoff-Bulman (1978). 'Lottery Winners and Accident Victims: Is Happiness Relative?' Journal of Personality and Social Psychology, 36, pages 917–27.

[cxiv] M. L. Richins, and S. Dawson (1992). 'A Consumer Values Orientation for Materialism and Its Measurement: Scale Development and Validation'. Journal of Consumer Research, 19 (3), pages 303–16.

[cxv] Kahneman, D., & Deaton, A. (2010). High income improves evaluation of life but not emotional well-being. Proceedings of the National Academy of Sciences, 107, 16489-16493.

[cxvi] E. W. Dunn, L. Aknin and M. I. Norton (2008). 'Spending Money on Others Promotes Happiness'. Science, 319, pages 1687–88.

[cxvii] Ashley V. Whillans, Elizabeth W. Dunn, Paul Smeets, Rene Bekkers, and Michael I. Norton "Buying time promotes happiness" PNAS vol. 114 no. 32 pp 8523–8527, doi: 10.1073/pnas.1706541114

[cxviii] F. Strack, L. L. Martin and S. Stepper (1988). 'Inhibiting and Facilitating Conditions of the Human Smile: A Nonobstrusive Test of the Facial Feedback Hypothesis'. Journal of Personality and Social Psychology, 54, pages 768–77.

[cxix] Dimberg U1, Thunberg M, Elmehed K. "Unconscious facial reactions to emotional facial expressions." Psychol Sci. 2000 Jan;11(1):86-9. DOI: 10.1111/1467-9280.00221

[cxx] T. A. Roberts and Y. Arefi-Afsha (2007). 'Not All Who Stand Tall Are Proud: Gender Differences in the Propioceptive Effects of Upright Posture'. Cognition and Emotion, 21, pages 714–27.

[cxxi] Erik Peper, PhD and I-Mei Lin "Increase or Decrease Depression: How Body Postures Influence Your Energy Level" *Biofeedback* Volume 40, Issue 3, pp. 125–130 DOI: 10.5298/1081-5937-40.3.01

cxxii "How to Improve Your Posture WikiHow accessed at https://www.wikihow.com/Improve-Your-Posture on 7 Dec 2017

cxxiii Jonathan M. Adler, Hal E. Hershfield "Mixed Emotional Experience Is Associated with and Precedes Improvements in Psychological Well-Being" *PLoS ONE* 7(4) 23 April 2012 DOI: doi.org/10.1371/journal.pone.0035633

cxxiv Hal E. Hershfield, Susanne Scheibe, Tamara L. Sims, and Laura L. Carstensen "When Feeling Bad Can Be Good: Mixed Emotions Benefit Physical Health Across Adulthood" Soc Psychol Personal Sci. 2013 Jan; 4(1): 54–61. DOI: 10.1177/1948550612444616

cxxv James H Fowler, Nicholas A Christakis, "Dynamic spread of happiness in a large social network: longitudinal analysis over 20 years in the Framingham Heart Study" *BMJ* 2008;337:a2338

cxxvi Ryan T. Howell David Chenot Graham Hill Colleen J. Howell "Momentary Happiness: The Role of Psychological Need Satisfaction" *Journal of Happiness Studies* March 2011, Volume 12, Issue 1, pp 1–15

cxxvii Kurtz, J. L. (2008). Looking to the future to appreciate the present: The benefits of perceived temporal scarcity. Psychological Science, 19, 1238-1241.

cxxviii Andrew Lepp Jacob E. Barkley Aryn C. Karpinski "The relationship between cell phone use, academic performance, anxiety, and Satisfaction with Life in college students" Computers in Human Behavior Volume 31, February 2014, Pages 343-350 https://doi.org/10.1016/j.chb.2013.10.049

cxxix Andrew Lepp Jacob E. Barkley Aryn C. Karpinski "College students' cell phone use and attachment to parents and peers" *Computers in Human Behavior* Volume 64, November 2016, Pages 401-408

cxxx Steve Baskin "Reasons Cell Phone Usage Reduces Happiness" Psychology Today 22 Jan 2014 access at https://www.psychologytoday.com/blog/smores-and-more/201401/reasons-cell-phone-usage-reduces-happiness on 8 Dec 2017

cxxxi Glued to Your Cell Phone? Research Suggests It May Reduce Your Physical Activity and Fitness accessed at https://www.kent.edu/kent/news/glued-your-cell-phone-research-suggests-it-may-reduce-your-physical-activity-and-fitness on 8 Dec 2017

cxxxii Florence Williams "How Just 15 Minutes in Nature Can Make You Happier" *Time* 7 February 22017 accessed at http://time.com/4662650/nature-happiness-stress/on 8 Dec 2017

cxxxiii Mauss, I. B., Savino, N. S., Anderson, C. L., Weisbuch, M., Tamir, M., & Laudenslager, M. L. (2012). "The pursuit of happiness can be lonely" *Emotion*, 12(5), 908-912. DOI: 10.1037/a0025299q

29889185R00063

Made in the USA
Columbia, SC
24 October 2018